F
Sim

Simon, Norma
Go away, Warts!

#9.08

DATE DUE			
FE 8'88	NOV 23 '88		
JE 14 '88	JY 24 '05		
OC 12 '88	AP 14 '16		
AG 12 '89			
JA 22 '90			
MY 8 '90			
JY 26 '90			
AG 21 '90			
FE 2 '91			
JY 15 '91			
SE 18 '91			
DE 3 '91			

MEDIALOG
Alexandria, Ky 41001

GO AWAY, WARTS!

NORMA SIMON

Pictures by Susan Lexa

ALBERT WHITMAN & COMPANY, CHICAGO

For Wendy, with many loving memories.

Library of Congress Cataloging in Publication Data

Simon, Norma.
   Go away, warts!

   (A Concept book)
   SUMMARY: Freddie is embarrassed by his ugly warts
and puzzled by their seemingly mysterious disappearance.
   [1. Warts — Fiction]   I. Lexa, Susan.   II. Title.
PZ7.S6053Go   [Fic]   79-28534
ISBN 0-8075-2970-2

Dear Reader,

When I mention warts, the first thing most people say is, "YUUUCK!" But, as soon as we talk a little more, people are eager to tell me about their wart "remedies."

Raw potatoes, colored juice, copper pennies, red silk thread, podophyllin, vitamins, saliva, garlic, celandine, rags rubbed on warts and buried at a crossroad—the list of "cures" goes on and on. Each person assures me that a particular cure really works on his or her warts.

Well, whatever works or doesn't, if you have warts, you're probably unhappy about them, just as Fred is in this story. Don't worry—you can be sure that warts eventually go away as mysteriously and unexpectedly as they appear. Family doctors and skin doctors can help if your warts bother you.

Maybe this book will help people of all ages talk about warts, laugh about warts, and exchange cures for them. I'd love to hear what works on your warts.

Norma Simon
Box 428
South Wellfleet, MA
02663

Ever had warts?

Last year a girl in my class named Sheila Francis had
them. The other kids sure made fun of her. Nobody
even wanted to take her milk money because it might
have touched her warts!

I felt sorry for Sheila. I don't know what happened
to her warts because her father got a new job and she
moved away.

I'd forgotten all about Sheila's warts until two little bumps popped out on one of *my* hands. Those bumps grew and grew. Pretty soon they had black specks on them, like pepper sprinklings.

You bet I knew what they were!

Those warts really bugged me. The bigger they grew, the more I kept rubbing them. My fingers looked all lumpy. The warts got rough and hard on top. Sometimes I wanted to pick them right off, like old scabs, but I didn't.

I didn't tell anybody I had warts. I sort of kept my hand out of the way so nobody would notice my fingers. But I asked around about warts, pretending I was just curious. Nobody, not even Grandpa, knew for sure how to cure them.

When I asked Grandpa about warts, he just laughed. "Never had them myself, Fred," he said, "but when I was about your size my friend Vinnie was covered with them."

"What did he do?" I asked.

"Somebody told Vinnie to go see an old lady up on Seir Hill. She was supposed to have 'The Power.' You know, magic. Sure enough, first full moon after Vinnie went up to her place those warts were bouncing off his hands like hailstones off a barn roof."

"Did his warts ever come back?"

"I forgot all about them until we were grown-up, and I was best man at Vin's wedding. Well, I was watching his hands when he put the ring on Jo's finger. And you know what, Fred? Vin's fingers were smooth as mine! Guess his warts disappeared for good."

I wished I could go see that old lady. But if she was old when Grandpa was a boy, she probably wasn't still alive. My grandpa is a pretty old man.

"What did the old lady do to Vinnie?" I asked Grandpa.

He laughed. "Beats me. She just made those warts go away, that's all I know."

So you can see Grandpa wasn't much help. I couldn't even tell if I was supposed to believe that story about Vinnie!

My Aunt Eulalia didn't help much, either.

Aunt Eulalia has so many aches and pains she keeps a box of medicines on her kitchen table all the time. I figured she might know something about warts, so one Saturday I took a bus out to the country to see her.

Aunt Eulalia grows herbs and weeds, and she's always cooking some soup on the back of her stove. She says all those vegetables and things keep a person healthy, but they don't seem to help her much.

When I got to Aunt Eulalia's, she was brewing some funny-smelling tea. I asked her what she knew about warts.

"Wa-arts?" she said in that moany way she has. "Well, we used to say frogs and toads give a person warts. I don't know if that's true, but I'd never touch those slimy things the way you do, Fred. You got warts?"

I wasn't ready for that. She looked at my hands, but I hid them in my pockets so she couldn't see anything.

Then she laughed. "How about a cup of herb tea, Freddie? I've heard herbs keep away warts. I always drink this herb tea and look—" she held out her hands—"no warts."

I laughed, too. I wasn't sure if she guessed I had warts or not. I tried to change the subject. "How've you been feeling, Aunt Eulalia?"

"Oh, poorly, same as always. Listen, Fred, take the kettle off when you hear it whistle. I'll be right back."

She headed outdoors and came back in a few minutes carrying a green weed with orange juice dripping out of the stem.

"I just read about this weed," she explained. "You're supposed to put some juice from it on your warts every day and they'll disappear."

Aunt Eulalia poured me a cup of tea. "Now try this —it might help keep warts away, too."

The tea was awful, all minty and musty. I sipped a little. Then I put in lots of honey and drank the rest. I didn't want to hurt Aunt Eulalia's feelings.

Before I got back on the bus she gave me a bag of vegetables to take home. The strange weed was on top.

"Well," she said with a wink, "we won't have to worry about *you* getting warts!"

The weed was wilted when I got home, so I threw it away. And I decided I wouldn't ask any more questions about warts. Someone might get suspicious.

But my wart problem was getting worse. One day
in school that awful Ellie Frank caught me looking
down at my hand.

"Hey, Freddie," she whispered. "Have you got warts?
My brother Hank has them. They're disgusting. Let's see."
She made a grab for my hand.

I hid it behind my back. "None of your business,"
I told Ellie.

"My brother put medicine on his warts. It burned."
She tried to grab my hand again.

I was getting angry. "I hope you catch them
from him!"

"That's a mean thing to say. I just might tell
everyone about your warts," she said, sticking her nose
in the air. "I just might."

I didn't know if Ellie would keep her mouth shut or not. That made me worry. And the warts were getting to be more and more trouble. They'd catch on things. They were bloody and ugly around the edges. I hated them.

The next thing I knew, my mother got this worried look. "What's that on your hands?" she asked.

"Where?" I said.

"You've been rubbing something, Fred. Let me have a look."

"Warts, Ma," I said. Actually, it was a relief to tell her. "There used to be just two. Now I've got three on the same hand." I held up my warty fingers.

"I tell you what, Fred, next time we go to the clinic to see Dr. Joyce, let's ask her about the warts."

I'd never thought about asking the doctor. "When, Ma?"

"The baby's due for her regular checkup next Thursday. You come, too."

My dad looked at my hand. "Why don't you just wait, Libby? The warts might go away by themselves. Mine did when I was a kid."

"Oh, as long as I'm going anyway, I might as well take Fred. You can see he's upset."

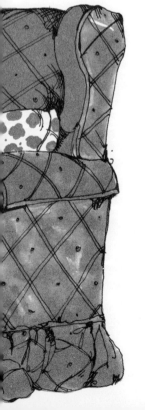

So Thursday after school my mother and the baby
and I went downtown to the clinic.

After Dr. Joyce had examined our baby, I showed
her my warts. I didn't mind. We've been coming to the
clinic to see her ever since I was a baby. Dr. Joyce was
even here when my mother was a little girl. I guess
that must mean she's an old lady, but she doesn't seem
old. Do you know what I mean? Her eyes are always
laughing. She doesn't walk as if she's old, either, the way
Aunt Eulalia does.

The doctor held my hand and looked at the warts
over her little half glasses. I wished I'd cleaned my
fingernails before we came. She looked at every wart
carefully.

"Warts are funny things, Freddie," she said. "We know they begin with viruses, the way colds do. But nobody knows yet why some people get them and some people don't."

"My dad said his warts went away by themselves," I said.

"Sometimes that happens. But, as long as your warts are still growing, I'd like you to try some vitamin A pills. Sometimes, just sometimes, vitamin A seems to work on warts. I don't mean the ordinary amount of vitamin A you get in foods—it would take a whole truckload of carrots to hold the vitamin A in one of these pills."

She gave me a pack of yellow pills. "Take these samples, and here's a prescription for more. Let me know if anything happens in about eight weeks. If the vitamin A doesn't work, we'll try something else."

I took a pill as soon as we got home. It was big enough to choke a horse. I swallowed it with a big glass of water. Then I took another glassful to wash it all the way down.

I was pretty good about taking those vitamins for the first few weeks, even though my warts looked just the same. Then I started making up excuses like "in a little while" or "later" when Mom gave me a pill. The vitamins didn't seem to be doing any good, anyway. And I just hated swallowing those huge horse things.

I'd stick the vitamins up on my dresser or in a drawer and pretty soon I'd forget all about them. Especially when Mom didn't ask, "Did you take your vitamins, Fred?" I guess I took them most of the time because Mom was always reminding me, but lots of days I forgot.

Then my cousin Jud came up from Boston for his
vacation. This was the first time Jud had ever come
without his whole family. We could do lots of things
just because Jud's older and my mom trusts him.

Jud makes jokes about everything, but not mean
jokes. I'd think about my warts everytime they started
bleeding a little. I'd tell myself I'd better take those
pills. Then Jud would start telling me something
funny, and I'd forget again. You know how that is?

A few days after Jud came, I showed him my warts.

"Hey, Fred, I never even noticed." He didn't say "yuck" or make fun of me. That's the kind of guy Jud is.

I told him about Grandpa's friend Vinnie and the old lady on Seir Hill.

"Maybe Grandpa was fooling you," Jud said. "You know how he is."

"Well, maybe. But I wish we could go see that old lady, just the same."

"We can't find a dead old lady," Jud said.
"Look—I'll try a little Abracadabra on your warts. It
can't hurt."

Jud turned out the lights. He looked very serious
and reached for my hand. His voice got slow and
mysterious. "I—have—the—Power. The Power to heal
your warts. Abracadabra! Go away, warts. GO AWAY,
WARTS! Away . . . far, far away! No more warts . . .
Shaazam!"

It was kind of spooky. But when we turned the lights back on, Jud laughed and I laughed, too. It was spooky and silly all at the same time.

Before we went to bed, I took another horse pill. I figured that wouldn't hurt, either.

"Wouldn't it be something if those warts did come off now?" I said to Jud.

"Something's got to work," Jud said.

The next Sunday Jud left for Boston. The whole family was standing by his bus, and I started to shake his hand. All of a sudden I got scared he might get my warts if he touched them. I pulled my hand back, but it was too late. Jud grabbed it.

"I had a great time, Fred. Maybe your folks will let you visit me real soon."

I dropped his hand as if it were red hot.

"What's wrong?" Jud said.

"My warts! You might catch them!"

I held out my warty hand. Jud looked at it and I looked at it and we both looked again. No warts! I held out my other hand. The right hand was as smooth as the left. I couldn't even tell where the warts used to be.

The bus driver yelled to Jud to get on, so he had to go. He waved goodbye from the window, and the bus drove off.

I was still looking at my hands. I couldn't believe my own eyes.

My mom was as surprised as I was. "Look at that," she said to Dad. "Fred's warts are all gone. They were right here, and now they're gone!"

"How do you explain it?" my father asked, touching my smooth hand.

For a minute I thought maybe this was all a dream. Maybe I'd wake up and the warts would be right back where they used to be.

Mom shook her head. "See? Dr. Joyce knew what to do. Vitamin A worked like a charm. That woman is my idea of a doctor."

I didn't have the heart to tell Mom about the pile of pills still in my room.

Now my mother goes around telling everyone about Dr. Joyce's marvelous remedy for warts. I don't know if those horse pills worked, but I'm so glad to get rid of my warts I don't care what made them disappear. I guess I'll never know.

Maybe Aunt Eulalia's terrible tea made them go away, but I don't think so. I never used the weed she gave me. Or maybe the warts disappeared all by themselves, the way my father said they would. It couldn't have been Jud's Abracadabra—he doesn't have the Power. Or does he?

Anyway, I've never gotten them again. And that's all I know about warts.